THE BASIC BABY FOOD COOKBOOK

Complete beginner guide to making baby food at home.
By Julianne E. Hood

Introduction by Brenda McGhee, M.D.
Design by Sheri Lawrence

AuthorHouse™
1663 Liberty Drive, Suite 200
Bloomington, IN 47403
www.authorhouse.com
Phone: 1-800-839-8640

AuthorHouse™ UK Ltd.
500 Avebury Boulevard
Central Milton Keynes, MK9 2BE
www.authorhouse.co.uk
Phone: 08001974150

First published by AuthorHouse 12/6/2006

ISBN: 978-1-4259-6067-4 (sc)

Library of Congress Number: 2006909967

Printed in the United States of America
Bloomington, Indiana

This book is printed on acid-free paper.

Foreward

If you were looking for a gourmet baby food cookbook with long complicated recipes...close this book and walk away. This book is filled with simple recipes made with basic foods. However, after mastering this simple process, **you** will be able to create and imagine hundreds of possible "gourmet" meal combinations and menu ideas that will not only be healthy for your child but flavorful as well.

The driving idea behind this little cookbook was to empower and encourage **all** parents to make simple, nutritious, time and cost-saving meals for their children.

As a new stay-at-home mom, I was overwhelmed with all the information and choices on how I should feed my baby. Recommendations came at me from baby food manufacturers, magazines, television, the web, parents and friends. My daughter's pediatrician even had the nerve to suggest I try making baby food at home. With my preference for cooking meals in twenty minutes or less, I seriously doubted my cooking experience was up to the task. And ... with a new baby ... where was I supposed to find the time?

However, I was curious so I did a bit of research. I read about homemade baby food on the web and talked to other moms. What I discovered stunned me!
Making homemade baby food:
- is easier than I ever imagined;
- allows me to control exactly what goes into the food, and thus, what goes into my baby;
- actually saves me time, energy and money.

I found that one cooking session could provide a month's supply of fruits and vegetables! Even my husband got into the act, helping plan our children's menus from the variety of baby foods I had made. My children loved and thrived on the food. Today, at ages 6 and 3, they are good eaters and happily sample new foods.

Whether you live in a rural area or an urban environment, you can make nutritious, affordable meals for your infant and toddler, even if you have no cooking experience. Each of the recipes in this book gives precise, step-by-step instructions and requires only ingredients commonly found at home.

Try a couple recipes. Compare them with the commercially jarred product. Don't hesitate to make a veggie because *you* don't like it. You may discover that the squash, or peas, or beets, you hated as a child didn't taste anything like the fresh veggies you prepare with the recipes in this book. You will notice that your homemade food has a brighter, truer color and tastes better than commercial baby food because it was quickly steamed in a small batch without added sugars, starch, salt or preservatives. You will understand that the very best food for your baby is the food you make yourself. If I could master this process, anyone can.

— J.H.

Introduction

Feeding your baby provides nutrition for his or her physical and mental growth, and watching your baby grow and thrive is one of life's most rewarding experiences. But feeding your baby during their growth from infant to toddler and helping him or her make the transition to table food — beyond mashed potatoes and McDonald's fries — can be a challenging part of parenting. Those tiny taste buds are set on HIGH perceiving flavors as intense. Even the infant rice cereal - the one we think tastes blah - is flavorful to your infant. Keeping that in mind, imagine the flavor a pea might present.

This is one reason this book is so important. By serving foods to your infant and toddler that you prepare, you know the peas look the way peas should look ... and that the peas taste the way peas should taste. You might even be surprised at how wonderfully delicious peas can taste when prepared as they are in this book. Do not be upset if your child does not like a food the first time it is introduced. Set the disliked food aside and try again another day. After a few tries, your child may readily accept it. The foods in this book are prepared and stored in small, individual servings that make this method of introducing food easy and economical.

The recipes in this book are simple and nutritious and put *you* in control of your child's nutrition. They are easy to prepare and offer you an opportunity to establish your child's healthy food preferences ... before they toddle off to nursery school for milk and cookies.

Remember to never force-feed your child or use food as either a reward or punishment. Always keep mealtimes happy and fun. Healthy eating habits now will help your child keep and maintain those habits when he gets older!

— Brenda McGhee, M.D.

Table of Contents

Feeding Your Child

Always consult your pediatrician
before feeding solid foods to your child.

Most children begin eating solid foods between four and sixth months of age, after their gag reflex has begun to recede. This is also the age at which a baby's iron stores from birth are starting to be depleted, making solid food feeding an important part of a baby's diet.

When introducing solid foods to your baby, offer plain, single-ingredient foods, usually infant cereals thinned with breast milk or formula, before adding pureed vegetables and fruits. While early solid foods teach a baby how to eat and offer good nutrition, they are meant to supplement breast milk/formula not replace it. Even at 12 months and beyond, milk/formula will remain an important part of your child's diet.

Introduce each new food at three to four day intervals. This allows you to observe your baby for food allergies, sensitivity or other reactions before introducing any other foods. If you notice skin rashes, diarrhea, unusual vomiting or irritability, contact your pediatrician and discontinue feeding that particular food. Possible common allergens to avoid before your child's first birthday include egg whites, peanut butter, honey, strawberries, raw tomatoes, fish, citrus and pineapple. Also, avoid any foods difficult to mash or swallow, which might pose a potential choking hazard (raisins, nuts, whole grapes, peanut butter, cherries with pits, popcorn, marshmallows, pretzels, chips and chunks of meat).

As your baby grows, so will his nutritional needs. Offering a variety of cereals, fruits and vegetables gives him important vitamins and minerals necessary for his developing body. Vitamin A, vitamin C, folic acid, potassium, iron, beta-carotene, B vitamins and dietary fiber are just some examples of the many important nutrients found in the variety of both fruits and vegetables suggested in this cookbook. Offering different kinds or combinations of fruits and vegetables will help your baby or toddler learn to enjoy a healthy, wide variety of foods.

For babies, breast milk/formula provides the bulk of their needed nutrition but the food pyramid offers good general guidelines to work on for ages 12 to 24 months. For older babies, the new food pyramid recommends at least 5 servings of fruits and vegetables, 2 servings of meats, and 6 to 11 servings of grains/cereals for all children ages 2 through age 6. The toddler meals and menu suggestions in this cookbook will help both you and your child meet those guidelines.

Getting Started

Getting Started

The cooking methods, which follow, are quick and easy. Do *not* be intimidated, especially if you do not consider yourself an accomplished cook. Each step-by-step recipe in this cookbook involves the short and **simple** process of cooking – or steaming— each food, straining (only if necessary), placing the food in ice cube trays (muffin cups for toddler meals), freezing, and then finally storing each food in labeled and sealed food freezer bags.

That's the entire process — nothing could be easier or healthier for your baby! Steam cooking fresh foods preserves many of the vitamins and minerals that might otherwise be boiled or cooked off. Steam cooking also preserves color and taste.

If you made each of only the basic fruits and vegetables listed on the following few pages you would have between 600 – 700 (1 ounce) individual servings in frozen storage. That is enough food to give your baby five daily servings of fruits and vegetables for almost 5 months! At that rate you would only have to remake those fruits and vegetables one additional time and that would be enough to last until your child is eating more grown up meals at 10 to 12 months. Not only will you save yourself money, but think of all the time and energy you save yourself. Preparing to make, store and serve your own baby food is deceptively easy. Besides using your own common sense in fruit/vegetable selection have the following items handy for baby food preparation:

What You Need

- **Ice cube trays**
  Several sets of both small and large trays will allow you to prepare several foods at one time. Smaller cubes (1 ounce or less), are more appropriate for a beginning eater. Larger cubes (1-2 ounce) will more easily satisfy the experienced eater.

- **Muffin/Cupcake baking pans** (for toddler meals)

- **Food processor** (6 to 10 cup capacity)

- **4 quart-8 quart lidded pot**

- **Steamer basket**
  (should fit into the 4 quart or 8 quart pot)

- **Metal strainer**

- **Wooden mixing spoon**

- **Spatula**

- **Freezer storage bags** (one gallon and quart size)

- **Permanent marker**

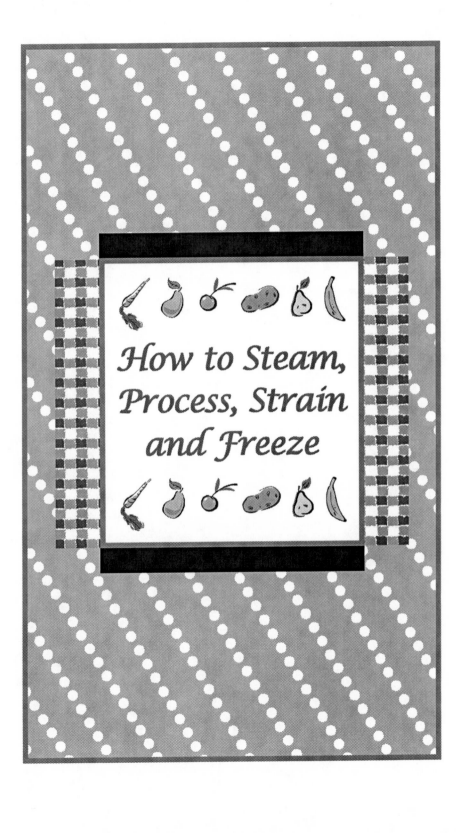

How to Steam, Process, Strain and Freeze

How to Steam, Process, Strain, and Freeze

Most recipes in this cookbook call for foods to be steam cooked.

Carefully wash all produce and fruit with a commercially available safe fruit/vegetable wash prior to use. Be sure the produce you use does not contain added spices/salt/sugar or starch, nor should you add, "spice," salt or any other additives to your baby food. Place your steamer basket in your pot, and fill the pot just until water touches the bottom of your steamer basket. Fill basket with food to be steamed. Close the lid securely. There should be less than one-inch space between the basket edge and pot (to prevent food from becoming lost in the water underneath).

Helpful Tips:
- Always monitor water level in steamer. If food becomes scorched (cooks without water) in steamer because water ran low, discard food, wash all utensils and begin again with fresh produce.
- Regularly monitor foods for "doneness." Hints for helping you tell when a food is done will be located in each recipe.
- Steamed/Cooked vegetables for these recipes will always be cooked through much softer than you would normally cook it for adult eaters. Softer foods process easier with less straining.
- Steamed fruits require less (sometimes *much* less) cooking time than most vegetables. Check your fruits often and be careful not to overcook, as some fruits can dissolve entirely in the steamer.
- Save any water remaining in your pot after steaming for use in processing the food. This boiled water is free of bacteria and contains vitamins/minerals and flavor from your steamed food.
- Allow all cooked foods to cool before processing.

Processing

Processing your foods with a conventional food processor helps insure that your food is of a consistency that your baby can easily swallow. When your recipe calls for processing your foods, use these simple steps and guidelines to make sure that your food is processed properly.

Transfer enough steamed and cooled food to processor to fill the food processor bowl 2/3 full. Overfilling your processor can result in poorly processed food and food leaking out underneath the lid. Begin by adding four ounces of cooled, reserved liquid from steaming pot to processor. Replace and lock lid on processor and process on low adding additional reserved liquid (up to 2 cups), if needed, so that processor runs smoothly. After water has been added, process on high until the food reaches a smooth, even consistency, pausing occasionally to scrape the sides of the bowl. Processing times will vary!

Helpful Tips:
- Process your food recipes in several batches if necessary to avoid overfilling your food processor.
- When adding water or reserved liquid to food processor, make sure processor is on low and add water slowly. Adding too much water will cause your food to be watery while adding too little will make your food more difficult to strain if preparing for a new eater. Remember – you can always add water but you cannot take it out!
- If you find you do not have enough reserved liquid to process the food, supplement with boiled water. Boil 3 to 4 cups of water for 5 minutes and allow it to cool before using.
- Older, more experienced eaters enjoy more texture in their foods and therefore their foods require less processing and less water. When you *re-make* a vegetable or fruit recipe for a more experienced eater, lower your processing time and do not strain. Add as much texture as your baby can safely and easily swallow. More texture also provides more interest!

Straining

For new eaters, food will need to be strained after processing.

Add processed food in batches to your metal wire strainer. Push your food through with a spatula discarding remaining pulp, lumps, seeds, peel or any other impurities. Be aware of choking risks! Even for experienced eaters enjoying textured, unstrained food, look for and remove large lumps, stems, seeds, peel or other impurities.

Freezing

For Infants: Spoon strained food into ice cube trays. Do not overfill because overfilled trays make frozen cubes hard to remove. After filling, tap the tray gently on even surface to remove air bubbles. Position filled trays in a single layer. If you need to stack trays, place a sheet of wax paper between trays so they don't stick together.

Freeze trays until food portions are solid throughout. Running warm water briefly along back of trays will make frozen cubes easier to remove. Place frozen cubes of food in freezer bag; label bag with the name of the food and the date it was prepared. Your frozen, properly stored food should last at least three months in your freezer.

For easy thawing, place cubes in small lidded plastic containers in your refrigerator the night before you plan to serve the food. Throw away thawed unused food within 24 hours after feeding.

For Toddlers: Prepare your muffin tins for toddler meals by spraying the tins with a non-stick cooking spray. Fill each muffin cup 2/3 full. Freeze tins until food portions are solid throughout. Run warm water briefly along back of tins to facilitate removal. Place frozen portions in a freezer bag labeled with the name of the food and the date it was prepared.

Four to Six Months

(Cereals)

Four to Six Months

Check with your pediatrician before introducing any food. Most pediatricians will recommend cereal as the first solid food to feed you infant. Do not be discouraged if your baby turns his nose up at his first taste. This does not mean that he does not like your food! Continue offering tastes of the new food over time. It may take your baby days to get used to the taste/texture of a new food and he may only eat small tastes or a spoonful at a sitting.

First Cereals

Rice, oatmeal, cracked wheat and barley cereals can all be found in the baby food aisle of your local supermarket but they can **also** be found in the regular breakfast food or organic foods aisle as well, usually at a **lower** cost per serving. Using the following recipes, you can easily turn wholesome "adult" variety cereals into "baby" cereals. I advise against making your baby's "first" cereal from the raw grain product because the self-processing of grains sometimes leads to small inconsistencies, lumps that can cause choking. In other words, don't buy long grain rice, rather a rice cereal; don't buy rolled oats, rather quick cooking oats. Once your child has mastered cereals and first foods, raw grain cereals that you process yourself not only taste better but also can be much cheaper. In addition, many processed grain cereals contain additives, frequently soy, which is important to know about in case your child has a soy allergy. Rice cereal has long been the first food recommended for most beginning eaters because it tends to be more hypo-allergenic.

Rice/Oatmeal or Barley Cereal

1 cup raw cereal (oatmeal quick oats, rice cereal or barley cereal)

Process dry, raw cereal in food processor until it reaches a fine consistency. Approximately 2-3 minutes on low speed. Empty into zip lock food storage bag or air tight container. Label and date.

To prepare: mix 1 tablespoon cereal to $\frac{1}{4}$ cup breast milk/formula and cook on low heat in small saucepan until liquid is absorbed and cereal is soft. Cool. Add additional breast milk/formula for desired consistency. (More liquid for less experienced babies.) You may substitute distilled or boiled water for breast milk/formula.

. . . .

Cracked Wheat Cereal

** Wheat sensitivity is common among small children. Do not introduce wheat into your child's diet before checking with your pediatrician. **

1 cup raw cracked wheat
1 food storage bag (quart size)

Process cracked wheat dry in food processor until fine consistency. Approximately 2-3 minutes on low speed. Empty into quart food storage bag or air tight container. Label and date.

To prepare: mix 1 tablespoon cereal to $\frac{1}{4}$ cup breast milk/formula and cook over low head in small saucepan until the liquid is absorbed and cereal is soft. Cool. Add additional breast milk/ formula for desired consistency. (More liquid for less experienced babies.) You may substitute distilled or boiled water for breast milk/formula.

. . . .

Cream of Wheat
(purchase adult 2 $\frac{1}{2}$ minute variety)
** Wheat sensitivity is common among small children. Do not introduce wheat into your child's diet before checking with your pediatrician. **

No processing needed. Use only for experienced cereal-eating babies. Do not add sugar/salt/butter or other spices. To serve, cook on low heat in small saucepan 1 part cereal to 3 parts breast milk/formula/water until soft. Cool. Add breast milk/formula/ water for desired consistency.

Six to Ten Months

(Vegetables)

Six to Ten Months

Because fruits have more natural sugar content than vegetables, and some children — if offered a choice — would choose a more sugary fruit over a less sweet vegetable, we suggest offering vegetables first. This allows your child to experience and enjoy a wide variety of flavors and textures in vegetables before experiencing the natural sugars found in fruits.

Vegetables

. . . .

Green Peas

Peas are a good source of vitamin C, thiamin, niacin, vitamin B6, magnesium, phosphorous, copper and manganese, and folate. Your baby food peas will have a beautiful, bright green color and rich taste.

4-6 cups fresh green peas or frozen peas
Water

Add the peas to your steamer basket. Cover and steam until done. (Peas are done when they can be easily smashed between your fingers.) Remove from pan to cool, reserving liquid. Transfer cooled peas to food processor along with 4 ounces ($\frac{1}{2}$ cup) of reserved liquid. Process until peas reach a smooth consistency adding additional reserved liquid slowly as needed (up to 2 cups using boiled water if there is not enough reserved liquid). If feeding to an inexperienced eater, strain carefully. Transfer strained peas to clean ice cube trays, being careful not to overfill. Freeze. When frozen solid, twist cubes from ice cube trays and place in a labeled and dated food storage freezer bag. Place filled bag in freezer.

Makes approximately 28-42 cubes/servings. (Store no more than 3 months.)

Green Beans

Green beans are a good source of thiamin, riboflavin, folate, calcium, iron, magnesium and potassium, and a very good source of dietary fiber, vitamin A, vitamin C and manganese. Your baby food green beans will have a pretty, light green color.

4-6 cups fresh green beans, *washed, ends and strings removed, cut or break in half* or frozen green beans
Water

Add green beans to your steamer basket. Cover and steam until done. (Green beans are done when can be easily smashed between your fingers.) Remove beans from pot to cool, reserving liquid. Transfer cooled beans to food processor along with 4 ounces of reserved liquid. Process until beans reach a smooth consistency, slowly adding more reserved liquid as needed (up to 2 cups using boiled water if there is not enough reserved liquid). If feeding to an inexperienced eater, strain carefully. Transfer strained green beans to clean ice cube trays, being careful not to overfill. Freeze. When frozen solid, twist cubes from ice cube trays and place in labeled and dated food storage freezer bag. Place bag in freezer.

Makes approximately 28-42 cubes/servings. (Store no more than 3 months.)

Carrots

Carrots are a good source of vitamin C, vitamin B6, potassium and copper, and a very good source of dietary fiber, vitamin A, vitamin K and manganese. Your baby food will have a bright orange color and fantastic intense carrot taste.

4-6 cups fresh peeled, chunked carrots, *ends removed (The peeled, fresh baby carrots readily available in bags may be used but they are not as flavorful and are tougher to process.)*
Water

Add carrots to your steamer basket. Cover and steam until done. (Carrots are done when they can be easily smashed between your fingers.) Remove from pot, reserving liquid. Transfer cooled carrots to food processor along with 4 ounces of reserved liquid. Process until carrots reach a smooth consistency, slowly adding reserved liquid as needed (up to 2 cups using boiled water if there is not enough reserved liquid). If feeding to an inexperienced eater, strain carefully. Transfer strained carrots to clean ice cube trays, being careful not to overfill. Freeze. When frozen solid, twist cubes from ice cube trays and place in labeled and dated food storage freezer bag. Place bag in freezer.

Makes approximately 28-42 cubes/servings. (Store no more than 3 months.)

Butternut Squash

Butternut Squash is a good source of vitamin E, thiamin, niacin, vitamin B6, folate, calcium and magnesium, and a very good source of vitamin A, beta-carotene, vitamin C, potassium and manganese. Your baby food squash will have a soft yellow-orange color and a muted squash flavor.

1 medium butternut squash, *washed*
Water

Cut squash in half, scraping out seeds. Cut squash halves into 4 or 5 large pieces. Arrange squash pieces evenly in steamer basket. Cover and steam until done. Steam squash until flesh and skin pierce easily with a fork. (TIP: Some foods take longer to steam. Monitor water level in bottom of pot and add more when low to prevent scorching.) When squash pieces are uniformly soft and cooked throughout, remove from heat and let cool reserving liquid. Scrape squash flesh from skin, discarding skins. Add squash to food processor along with 4 ounces of reserved cooking liquid. Process until squash reaches a smooth consistency adding reserved liquid slowly as needed (up to 2 cups using boiled water if there is not enough reserved liquid). If feeding to an inexperienced eater, strain carefully. Transfer strained squash to clean ice cube trays, being careful not to overfill. Freeze. When frozen solid, twist cubes from ice cube trays and place in labeled and dated food storage freezer bag. Place bag in freezer.

Makes approximately 28-42 cubes/servings. (Store for no more than 3 months.)

Sweet Potatoes

Sweet potatoes are a good source of dietary fiber, vitamin B6 and potassium, and a very good source of vitamin A, beta-carotene, vitamin C and manganese. Your sweet potato baby food will have an intense dark orange color.

4 large or 5 medium sized Sweet Potatoes/Yams, *washed*
Water

Preheat oven to 350. Pierce sweet potatoes with a fork or knife and place on a shallow baking pan in oven. Bake for approximately 45 minutes until uniformly soft and cooked throughout. (Potatoes are done when they can be easily pierced with a fork.) Remove potatoes from oven and let cool. While the sweet potatoes are baking, boil approximately 3-4 cups of water for at least 5 minutes, let cool. When sweet potatoes are cool enough to handle, cut each potatoes in half and scrape flesh away from skin and into food processor (discard skin). Add 4 ounces of the boiled water and process until sweet potatoes reach a smooth consistency, slowly adding additional boiled water as needed. If feeding to an inexperienced eater, strain carefully. Transfer strained sweet potatoes to clean ice cube trays, being careful not to overfill. Freeze. When frozen solid, twist cubes from ice cube trays and place in labeled and dated food storage freezer bag. Place bag in freezer.

Makes approximately 28-42 cubes/servings. (Store for no more than 3 months.)

Pumpkin

Pumpkin is a good source of vitamin E, thiamin, niacin, vitamin B6, folate, Iron, magnesium and phosphorous, and a very good source of dietary fiber, vitamin A, beta-carotene, vitamin C, riboflavin, potassium, copper and manganese. Your baby food pumpkin will have a rich orange color and a concentrated earthy flavor.

1 small - medium pumpkin, *washed*
Water

Cut pumpkin in half, scraping out seeds. Cut pumpkin halves into 4 or 5 large pieces. Arrange pumpkin pieces evenly in steamer basket. Steam pumpkin until flesh and skin pierces easily with a fork. (TIP: Some foods take longer to steam. Monitor water level in bottom of pot and add more when low to prevent scorching.) When pumpkin pieces are uniformly soft and cooked throughout, remove from heat and let cool, reserve liquid. Scrape pumpkin flesh from skin into bowl of food processor (discard skins). Add 4 ounces of reserved liquid and process until pumpkin reaches a smooth consistency, slowly adding reserved liquid as needed (up to 2 cups using boiled water if there is not enough reserved liquid). If feeding to an inexperienced eater, strain carefully. Transfer strained pumpkin to clean ice cube trays, being careful not to overfill. Freeze. When frozen solid, twist cubes from ice cube trays and place in labeled and dated food storage freezer bag. Place bag in freezer.

Makes approximately 28-42 cubes/servings. (Store for no more than 3 months.)

Potatoes

Potatoes are very low in saturated fat, cholesterol and sodium and a good source of dietary fiber, vitamin C, vitamin B6, iron and manganese. They are also a very good source of copper. Your potato baby food will have a pleasing white color and a soft light flavor.

5-7 large or medium sized baking potatoes, *washed*
Water

Preheat oven to 350. Pierce potatoes with a fork or knife and place on a shallow baking sheet in oven. Bake for approximately 45 minutes. (Potatoes are done when they can be easily pierced with a fork.) When potatoes are uniformly soft and cooked throughout, remove from oven and let cool. While the potatoes are baking, boil approximately 3-4 cups of water for at least 5 minutes and let cool. Cut potatoes in half and scrape flesh away from skin into bowl of food processor (discard skins). Add 4 ounces of boiled water to processor and process until potatoes reach a smooth consistency, slowly adding additional boiled water as needed. If feeding to an inexperienced eater, strain carefully. Transfer strained potatoes to clean ice cube trays, being careful not to overfill. Freeze. When frozen solid, twist cubes from ice cube trays and place in labeled and dated food storage freezer bag. Place bag in freezer.

Makes approximately 28-42 cubes/servings. (Store for no more than 3 months.)

Zucchini

Zucchini is a good source of thiamin, riboflavin, niacin, vitamin B6 and phosphorous, and a very good source of dietary fiber, vitamin A, vitamin C, vitamin K, folate, magnesium, potassium, copper and manganese. This terrific baby food has a soft green color and a fresh light squash flavor.

1 large or 2 medium zucchini, *washed (you do not need to remove seeds unless zucchini is more than 3 inches in diameter)*
Water

Remove ends and cut each zucchini in half; cut each half into 4 or 5 large pieces. Arrange zucchini pieces evenly in steamer basket. Steam zucchini until flesh and skin pierce easily with a fork. (TIP: Some foods take longer to steam. Monitor water level in bottom of pot and add more when low to prevent scorching.) When zucchini pieces are uniformly soft and cooked throughout, remove from heat and let cool reserving liquid. You may either place zucchini chunks directly into food processor or you can scrape zucchini flesh from skin (discard skin) before use. Add 4 ounces of reserved cooking liquid and process until zucchini reaches a smooth consistency, slowly adding reserved liquid as needed (up to 2 cups using boiled water if there is not enough reserved liquid). If feeding to an inexperienced eater, strain carefully. Transfer strained zucchini to clean ice cube trays, being careful not to overfill. Freeze. When frozen solid, twist cubes from ice cube trays and place in labeled and dated food storage freezer bag. Place bag in freezer.

Makes approximately 28-42 cubes/servings. (Store for no more than 3 months.)

Broccoli

Broccoli is a good source of Protein, vitamin E, thiamin, pantothenic acid, calcium, iron, magnesium and phosphorous, and a very good source of dietary fiber, vitamin A, vitamin C, vitamin K, riboflavin, vitamin B6, folate, potassium and manganese. Your broccoli baby food will be a lovely dark green color with a mellow pleasing flavor.

3 - 4 fresh broccoli crowns, *washed, cut into small chucks, large stem removed*
Water

Arrange broccoli in steamer basket. Steam until broccoli can be easily smashed between your fingers or pierced with a fork. Remove from heat to cool, reserving liquid. Transfer broccoli to food processor along with 4 ounces of reserved liquid. Process until broccoli reaches a smooth consistency, slowly adding additional reserved liquid as needed (up to 2 cups using boiled water if there is not enough reserved liquid). If feeding to an inexperienced eater, strain carefully. Transfer strained broccoli to clean ice cube trays, being careful not to overfill. Freeze. When frozen solid, twist cubes from ice cube trays and place in labeled and dated food storage freezer bag. Place bag in freezer.

Makes approximately 28-42 cubes/servings. (Store no more than 3 months.)

Cauliflower

Cauliflower is a good source of protein, thiamin, riboflavin, phosphorus and potassium, and a very good source of dietary fiber, vitamin C, vitamin K, vitamin B6, folate, pantothenic acid and manganese. This super food is a light milky color when processed and has a light barely-noticeable taste and flavor.

1 large fresh cauliflower head, *washed, broken into flowerets, large inner stem and leaves removed*
Water

Add 6-8 cups cauliflower to steamer basket. Steam until cauliflower can be easily smashed between your fingers or pierced with a fork. (TIP: Some foods take longer to steam. Monitor water level in bottom of pot and add more when low to prevent scorching.) When cauliflower is uniformly soft and cooked through, remove from heat and let cool, reserving liquid. Transfer cooled cauliflower to food processor along with 4 ounces of reserved liquid. Process until cauliflower reaches a smooth consistency, slowly adding additional reserved liquid as needed (up to 2 cups using boiled water if there is not enough reserved liquid). If feeding to an inexperienced eater, strain carefully. Transfer strained cauliflower to clean ice cube trays, being careful not to overfill. Freeze. When frozen solid, twist cubes from ice cube trays and place in labeled and dated food storage freezer bag. Place bag in freezer.

Makes approximately 28-42 cubes/servings. (Store no more than 3 months.)

Beets

Beets are a good source of dietary fiber, vitamin C, magnesium and potassium, and a very good source of folate and manganese. Your baby food will have an intense purple color and a slightly sweet, bright flavor.

SPECIAL NOTE: Because of the rich nature of beets and their high nitrate content, beets are not recommended for beginning eaters, under 6 months of age. For older eaters, continue to use the small ice cube trays for small vitamin-rich servings.

6 medium fresh beets, *peeled and cut into quarters (raw beets are much easier to peel)*
Water

Arrange beets evenly in steamer basket. Steam until beets can be easily pierced through with a fork. (TIP: Some foods take longer to steam. Monitor water level in bottom of pot and add more when low to prevent scorching.) When beets are uniformly soft and cooked throughout, remove from heat and let cool, reserving liquid. Transfer beets to food processor along with 4 ounces of reserved liquid. Process until beets reach a smooth consistency, slowly adding remaining reserved liquid as needed (up to 2 cups using boiled water if there is not enough reserved liquid). If feeding to an inexperienced eater, strain carefully. Transfer strained beets to clean ice cube trays, being careful not to overfill. Freeze. When frozen solid, twist cubes from ice cube trays and place in labeled and dated food storage freezer bag. Place bag in freezer.

Makes approximately 14-28 cubes/servings. (Store no more than 3 months.)

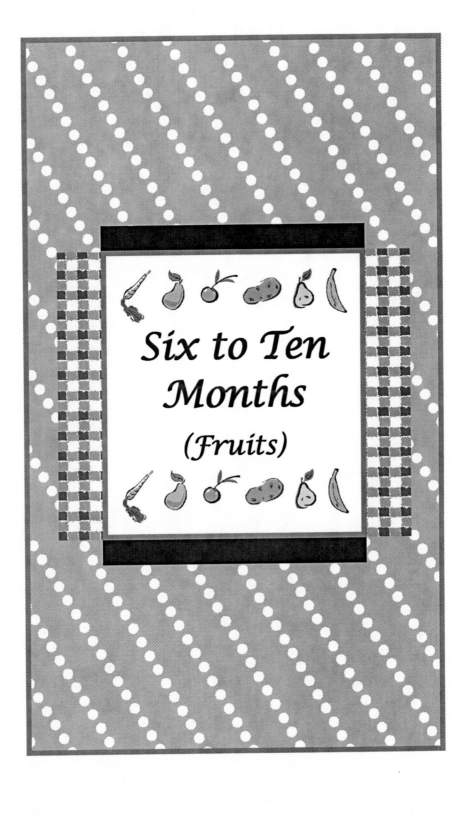

Six to Ten Months

(Fruits)

Fruits

. . . .

Apples

Apples are very low in saturated fat, cholesterol and sodium and are a good source of dietary fiber. Your apple baby food will have a muted light yellow color and a lovely smell and taste.

6-8 medium, washed Granny Smith/Jonathan or Gala apples (or any firm, flavorful cooking apple), *halved and cored*
Water

Arrange apple halves evenly in steamer basket. Steam apples until skin removes easily from fruit and flesh is uniformly soft. (TIP: Some foods take longer to steam. Monitor water level in bottom of pot and add more when low to prevent scorching.) Remove apples from heat, reserving liquid. When apples are cool, remove skin from fruit and discard skins. Transfer fruit to food processor along with 4 ounces of reserved liquid. Process until apples reach a smooth consistency, slowly adding additional reserved liquid as needed (up to 2 cups using boiled water if there is not enough reserved liquid). If feeding to an inexperienced eater, strain carefully. Transfer strained apples to clean ice cube trays, being careful not to overfill. Freeze. When frozen solid, twist cubes from ice cube trays and place in labeled and dated food storage freezer bag. Place bag in freezer.

Makes approximately 28-42 cubes/servings. (Store no more than 3 months.)

Pears

Pears are very low in saturated fat, cholesterol and sodium. They are a good source of vitamin C, and a very good source of dietary fiber. Your pear baby food will have a clean, off-white color and a fantastic bright flavor.

6 medium ripe pears (any variety), *washed, halved and cored*
Water

Arrange pears evenly in steamer basket. Steam pears until skin removes easily from fruit and flesh is cooked throughout. (TIP: Some foods take longer to steam. Monitor water level in bottom of pot and add more when low to prevent scorching.) Remove fruit from heat, reserving liquid. When fruit is cool, remove skins and discard. Transfer fruit to food processor along with 4 ounces of reserved liquid. Process until pears reach a smooth consistency, slowly adding additional reserved liquid as needed (up to 2 cups using boiled water if there is not enough reserved liquid). If feeding an inexperienced eater, strain carefully. Transfer strained pears to clean ice cube trays, being careful not to overfill. Freeze. When frozen solid, twist cubes from ice cube trays and place in labeled and dated food storage freezer bag. Place bag in freezer.

Makes approximately 28-42 cubes/servings. (Store no more than 3 months.)

Peaches

Peaches are a good source of dietary fiber, vitamin A, niacin and potassium, and a very good source of vitamin C. Your baby food will have an intense yellow-orange color and a delicious smell with rich flavor.

8 large or 9 medium sized, ripe peaches, *washed, halved and pits removed*
Water

Arrange peach halves evenly in steamer basket. Steam peaches until skin removes easily and flesh is uniformly cooked throughout. (TIP: Some foods take longer to steam. Monitor water level in bottom of pot and add more when low to prevent scorching.) Remove fruit from heat, reserving liquid. When fruit is cool, remove skins and discard. Transfer fruit to food processor along with 4 ounces of reserved liquid. Process until peaches reach a smooth consistency, slowly adding additional reserved liquid as needed (up to 2 cups using boiled water if there is not enough reserved liquid). If feeding to an inexperienced eater, strain carefully. Transfer strained peaches to clean ice cube trays, being careful not to overfill. Freeze. When frozen solid, twist cubes from ice cube trays and place in labeled and dated food storage freezer bag. Place bag in freezer.

Makes approximately 28-42 cubes/servings. (Store no more than 3 months.)

Apricots - Fresh

Apricots are a good source of dietary fiber, vitamin C, vitamin B6, Iron, potassium, copper and manganese, and a very good source of vitamin A. This great baby food will be a bright autumn, orange color with a heavenly smell and flavorful taste.

2 ½ - 3 pounds ripe apricots, *washed, pits removed*
Water

Arrange apricot halves evenly in steamer basket. Steam apricot halves until skin removes easily from fruit and flesh is uniformly soft and cooked throughout. (TIP: Some foods take longer to steam. Monitor water level in bottom of pot and add more when low to prevent scorching.) Remove fruit from heat, reserving liquid. When fruit is cool, remove skin and discard. Transfer fruit to food processor along with 4 ounces of reserved liquid. Process until apricots reach a smooth consistency, slowly adding additional reserved liquid as needed (up to 2 cups using boiled water if there is not enough reserved liquid). If feeding to an inexperienced eater, strain carefully. Transfer strained apricots to clean ice cube trays, being careful not to overfill. Freeze. When frozen solid, twist cubes from ice cube trays and place in labeled and dated food storage freezer bag. Place bag in freezer.

Makes approximately 14-28 cubes/servings. (Store no more than 3 months.)

Apricots - Canned

3, 15-ounce cans of apricot halves, *strained and rinsed, discard liquid in can*
Water

Arrange apricot halves evenly in steamer basket. Steam only until apricots are cooked throughout. Canned fruit does not usually contain skins. Remove fruit from heat, reserving liquid. When fruit is cool, transfer to bowl of food processor along with 4 ounces of reserved cooking liquid. Process until apricots reach a smooth consistency, slowly adding additional reserved liquid as needed (up to 2 cups using boiled water if there is not enough reserved liquid). If feeding to an inexperienced eater, strain carefully. Transfer strained apricots to clean ice cube trays, being careful not to overfill. Freeze. When frozen solid, twist cubes from ice cube trays and place in labeled and dated food storage freezer bag. Place bag in freezer.

Makes approximately 14-28 cubes/servings. (Store no more than 3 months.)

Bananas

Bananas are a good source of dietary fiber, vitamin C, potassium and manganese, and a very good source of vitamin B6. Your bananas will be creamy yellow with an unbeatable fresh flavor.

1 ripe banana, *peeled*

Mash banana well with a fork until consistency is creamy. Serve plain or added to whatever meal/cereal desired. Always serve fresh banana. Frozen, the flesh of a banana will turn unappetizingly black!

Plums

Plums are a good source of dietary fiber, vitamin A and vitamin K, and a very good source of vitamin C. Your plum baby food will be a light pink color with a tangy sweet flavor.

7-8 medium, ripe plums (black or red), *washed, halved, pits removed*
Water

Arrange plum halves evenly in steamer basket. Steam plums until skin removes easily from fruit and flesh is uniformly soft and cooked throughout. (TIP: Some foods take longer to steam. Monitor water level in bottom of pot and add more when low to prevent scorching.) Remove fruit from heat, reserving liquid. When fruit is cool, remove and discard skins. Transfer fruit to food processor, along with 4 ounces of reserved liquid. Process until fruit reaches a smooth consistency adding additional reserved liquid slowly as needed (up to 2 cups using boiled water if there is not enough reserved liquid). If feeding to an inexperienced eater, strain carefully. Transfer strained apricots to clean ice cube trays, being careful not to overfill. Freeze. When frozen solid, twist cubes from ice cube trays and place in labeled and dated food storage freezer bag. Place bag in freezer.

Makes approximately 28-42 cubes/servings. (Store no more than 3 months.)

Mango

Mangos are a good source of dietary fiber and vitamin B6, and a very good source of vitamin A and vitamin C. Mango baby food has a terrific bright dandelion yellow color and rich tropical sweet taste.

3-4 large ripe mangos.
Mangos have an extremely large, hard pit. Remove fruit from the pit by drawing your knife around the pit.
Water

Arrange mango pieces evenly in steamer basket. Steam mangos until skins are pierced easily with a knife and fruit is uniformly cooked throughout. (TIP: Some foods take longer to steam. Monitor water level in bottom of pot and add more when low to prevent scorching.) Remove from heat, reserving liquid. When cool, scrape fruit from skins; discard skins. Transfer fruit to food processor along with 4 ounces of reserved liquid. Process until mangos reach a smooth consistency, slowly adding additional reserved liquid as needed (up to 2 cups using boiled water if there is not enough reserved liquid). If feeding to an inexperienced eater, strain carefully. Transfer strained mangos to clean ice cube trays, being careful not to overfill. Freeze. When frozen solid, twist cubes from ice cube trays and place in labeled and dated food storage freezer bag. Place bag in freezer.

Makes approximately 28-42 cubes/servings. Freeze no longer than 3 months.

Blueberries/Raspberries/Blackberries

Berries are a good source of dietary fiber, and a very good source of vitamin C, vitamin K and manganese. Your berry baby food will have a deep blue/crimson/blue-black color and a tangy, bright taste.

1-2 quarts fresh Raspberries/Blueberries or Blackberries, *washed* (or frozen)
Water

Place washed fresh or frozen fruit in a 4-8quart pot. Add 2 cups of water and bring to a boil over low heat. Boil for approximately 5 minutes, stirring continuously until fruit breaks up and mashes easily. Remove pot from heat and let cool. Transfer cooked fruit and liquid to food processor. Process until berries reach a smooth consistency, slowly adding additional boiled water as needed. Strain carefully. Transfer strained berries to clean ice cube trays, being careful not to overfill. Freeze. When frozen solid, twist cubes from ice cube trays and place in labeled and dated food storage freezer bag. Place bag in freezer.

Makes approximately 14-28 cubes/servings. Freeze no longer than 3 months.

Prunes

Prunes are very low in saturated fat, cholesterol and sodium, a good source of dietary fiber, and a very good source of vitamin K.

NOTE: This baby food was one of my children's favorites! They were hooked on the lovely chocolate color and sweet rich flavor. This high fiber food also helps prevent or ease constipation.

1 large container of pitted prunes (unflavored), *carefully check each prune for pits*
Water

Place prunes in a 4-8 quart pot. Add enough water to cover prunes and bring to a boil over low heat. Boil for approximately 15-20 minutes, stirring continuously until fruit breaks up and mashes easily. Remove pot from heat and let cool. Transfer cooled fruit and liquid to food processor. Process on low for approximately 2 minutes adding additional boiled water if needed until fruit processes to a smooth consistency. Scrape sides of processor. Process on high for one additional minute. Transfer processed prunes to clean ice cube trays, being careful not to overfill. Process remaining cooked fruit in the same manner. Place ice cube trays in freezer on level surface. When frozen solid, twist cubes from ice cube trays and place in labeled and dated food storage freezer bag. Place bag in freezer.

Makes approximately 14-28 cubes/servings. Freeze no longer than 3 months.

Menu
Planning

Menu Planning

Having all of your prepared, natural baby foods stored in labeled freezer bags allows you to easily locate the fruits and vegetables for your child's daily menu. Placing each fruit or vegetable cube in a covered dish or half-pint storage container in your refrigerator the night before you plan to serve it, allows the food to thaw gradually so it will be fresh and ready to serve the next day. Once your child begins eating five servings or more of fruits or vegetables a day, extra covered dishes and/or small storage cups will come in handy.

Once your child has been introduced to the cereals, fruits and vegetables on the previous pages and have observed your child for possible allergic reactions, you can offer foods singly or in creative combinations. Menu extras on page 40 and sample menu recipes on pages 41-47 are offered to show additional combinations you might like to try with your baby.

When beginning to combine menu choices, have fun and do not be discouraged if your child does not take to a particular combination right away. As with plain fruits and vegetables, sometimes your child will need to taste the food a few times over the course of a few days to get used to its taste/texture.

Meal planning on-the-go is easy with your prepared frozen foods. For day trips, a small insulated lunchbox or cooler will keep your prepared foods cold until needed. For longer trips, add ice packs or storage bags filled with ice to your cooler to keep the foods frozen until you need them.

Menu Extras and Finger Foods

Look for these additional items to add to your experienced baby's diet to provide variety, interest, flavor and — most importantly — nutrition. These items are only to be added to your baby's diet after six months of age or when your baby can handle the consistency. Check with your pediatrician before adding any milk products to your baby's diet.

- Plain Yogurt (not vanilla, flavored, or low-fat)
- Cottage Cheese (small curd, you may wish to mash this a bit with a fork until your child gets used to the consistency)
- Pastina (stars pasta) You will find this in the boxed pasta aisle of your grocery store. Prepare pastina the same way you would baby cereal: 1 tablespoon pasta to $\frac{1}{4}$ cup water in a small saucepan. Bring to a boil on low heat until pasta is soft or water is absorbed. Cool and serve. *Variations*: mix with your child's favorite vegetable or two. Add a Tablespoon of cottage cheese.

When your child begins to show an interest in feeding himself/herself, you may consider adding the following finger foods to your child's menu or as a snack. These foods often provide good nutrition for your child as well. For variety you can mix any of your fruits/vegetables with these menu extras. Continue to follow the 3 to 4 day rule between the introduction of all new foods to your child and watch for the signs of allergic reaction. Also, never let your child eat finger foods unattended. Monitor your child closely while eating and always be on the lookout for the signs of choking.

- Rice Cakes (plain)
- Multi-grain Cheerios
- Shredded Cheese
- Zwieback
- Toast
- Arrowroot cookies

Sample Infant Meal Recipes

Offering your baby or toddler the plain version of fruits and vegetables you have made for them is important for the first few months. In fact, when young eaters are just starting out they may prefer their fruits and/or veggies individually. You may be feeding your child only one solid food per day for a few weeks before your begin adding these foods for a second feeding. Adding meals is a gradual process. It may be several months before your child works up to three or more meals per day including snacks. The following menu recipes are offered simply to spur your own creativity and to present menu ideas for when your older baby (older than six months) is ready for a bit more variety and meal variation in addition to your regular single-food servings.

Breakfasts

Blueberries and Cream Oatmeal

1 cube blueberries, *thawed*
1 tablespoon plain yogurt
Baby oatmeal cereal

Prepare your baby oatmeal cereal as usual. Add first two ingredients to cereal while warm. Use more or less blueberries to suit your child. Serve immediately. Discard leftovers. *Variation*: add mashed banana, prunes or apple.

Banana Cream of Rice Cereal

¼ mashed raw banana
1 tablespoon plain yogurt
Baby rice cereal

Prepare your baby rice cereal as usual. Add first two ingredients to cereal while warm. Use more or less mashed banana to suit your child. Serve immediately. Discard leftovers. *Variation*: add pear, any berry, prunes or apple.

Apple-Pear Cream of Wheat

1 cube apple, *thawed*
1 cube pear, *thawed*
Baby Cream of Wheat cereal

Prepare your baby Cream of Wheat cereal as usual. Add first two ingredients to cereal while warm. Serve immediately. Discard leftovers. *Variation*: add plum, peaches and/or one tablespoon of plain yogurt.

Peaches and Cream Cereal

1 cube peaches, *thawed*
1 tablespoon plain yogurt
Baby oatmeal cereal

Prepare your baby oatmeal cereal as usual. Add first two ingredients to cereal while warm. Serve immediately. Discard leftovers. *Variation*: add pear or apple.

"Pruney" Apple Breakfast

1 cube apple, *thawed*
1 cube prunes, *thawed*
1 tablespoon plain yogurt
Baby oatmeal cereal

Prepare your baby oatmeal cereal as usual. Add first three ingredients to cereal while warm. Serve immediately. Discard leftovers. *Variation*: substitute pear or berry cube for apple.

Mango Yogurt
(This one also makes a fantastic snack or dessert!)

1 cube mango, *thawed*
4 tablespoons plain yogurt

Mix first two ingredients and serve cold. Delicious! *Variation*: add any baby cereal.

Apricots and Cream Cracked Wheat Cereal

1 cube apricot, *thawed*
1 tablespoon plain yogurt
Baby Cracked Wheat cereal

Prepare your baby cracked wheat cereal as usual. Add first two ingredients to cereal while warm. Serve immediately. Discard leftovers. *Variation*: add mashed banana or apple.

Lunches

Peas-n-Carrots Cottage Cheese

1 cube carrots, *thawed*
1 cube green peas, *thawed*
2 tablespoons cottage cheese (small curd)

Mix all ingredients and serve immediately. Use more or less cottage cheese to suit your child's taste. Discard leftovers. *Variation*: add green beans, zucchini, cauliflower or butternut squash.

Butternut Squash Barley

1 cube squash, *thawed*
Baby barley cereal

Prepare your baby barley cereal as usual. Add squash to cereal while warm. Serve immediately. Discard leftovers. *Variation*: add apple, cauliflower, pumpkin or potato.

Pumpkin, Apple Cottage Cheese

1 cube pumpkin, *thawed*
1 cube apple, *thawed*
2 tablespoons cottage cheese

Mix all three ingredients and serve chilled. Discard leftovers. *Variation*: add squash or pear.

Broccoli, Cauliflower and Potato Medley

1 cube broccoli, *thawed*
1 cube cauliflower, *thawed*
1 cube potato, *thawed*

Mix all three ingredients and serve warmed. Discard leftovers.
Variation: add 1 tablespoon cottage cheese, or baby pasta.

Zucchini, Sweet Potato and Cauliflower Medley

1 cube zucchini, *thawed*
1 cube cauliflower, *thawed*
1 cube sweet potato, *thawed*

Mix all three ingredients and serve warmed. Discard leftovers.
Variation: substitute pumpkin for sweet potato. *Variation*: Add
1 tablespoon cottage cheese, or baby pasta.

Purple Cottage Cheese

1 cube beets, *thawed*
2 tablespoons cottage cheese (small curd)

Mix both ingredients together and serve immediately. Discard
leftovers. *Variation*: add potato or cauliflower.

Dinners

Carrot-Zucchini Pasta

1 cube carrot, *thawed*
1 cube zucchini, *thawed*
Prepared baby pasta (Pastina)

Prepare baby pasta as usual. Add first two ingredients while warm and serve immediately. Discard leftovers. *Variation*: add one tablespoon cottage cheese, cauliflower or green beans or substitute sweet potato or pumpkin for carrot.

Broccoli, Sweet Potato Barley

1 cube broccoli, *thawed*
1 cube cauliflower, *thawed*
1 cube potato, *thawed*

Mix all three ingredients and serve warmed. Discard leftovers. *Variation*: add one tablespoon cottage cheese, or baby pasta.

Pea, Carrot, Green Bean and Potato Medley

1 cube broccoli, *thawed*
1 cube cauliflower, *thawed*
1 cube potato, *thawed*

Mix all three ingredients and serve warmed. Discard leftovers. *Variation*: add squash, green beans or one tablespoon cottage cheese or baby pasta.

Vegetable Cheese Pasta

1 cube carrot, *thawed*
1 cube broccoli, *thawed*
1 cube cauliflower, *thawed*
1 tablespoon cottage cheese
Prepared baby pasta (Pastina)

Prepare baby pasta as usual. Add first four ingredients to pastina while warm and serve immediately. Discard leftovers. *Variation*: substitute sweet potato or pumpkin for carrot.

Ten to
Twenty
Months

Ten to Twenty Months

Fruits and Vegetables

The fruits and vegetables offered to your experienced baby are the same fruits and vegetables you prepared for your infant. However, cooking instructions for each fruit and vegetable will vary slightly as to the length of time that you process each item. You want fruits and veggies for the ten-to-twenty-month-old child to have a thicker, chunkier consistency which requires only half the processing time and slightly less water than was needed for the infant recipes. Experienced eaters are better at chewing and swallowing and like to practice their new skills on different textures However, even though you no longer have to strain foods, keep a lookout for overly large impurities, lumps, stems, seeds, peels or other inconsistencies in your processing that could be a choking hazard. Again, remember to wait 3 to 4 days between the introduction of new foods to your child and watch for any signs of allergic reaction.

Meats

You may prefer to make all your meats in the small ice cube trays, which will prevent expensive waste. One small cube of prepared meat constitutes one full serving and is usually more palatable to a new eater if mixed with one of his regular favorites. Boiled, steamed, roasted meats are preferable to any which are pan fried, micro waved (cooking results vary) or grilled.

Chicken, Turkey, Beef or Pork

Chicken is low in sodium, a good source of vitamin B6 and phosphorous, and a very good source of protein, niacin and Selenium. Turkey is also low in sodium, a good source of niacin, vitamin B6 and phosphorous, and a very good source of protein and Selenium. Ground chuck is low in sodium, a good source of niacin, vitamin B12, Zinc and Selenium. Roast pork is low in sodium, a good source of thiamin and niacin, and a very good source of protein and Selenium.

2 pounds, cooked, chicken breast, turkey breast, ground chuck or roast pork, *lean with all fat, skin, gristle, bones removed*
Water

Boil 3 to 4 cups of water on the stove for approximately 5 minutes, let cool. Chop or dice your cooked meat, removing any remaining skin, fat, gristle or bone. Place meat in food processor with 1 cup of boiled water. Process on low speed for approximately 2 minutes adding additional boiled water as needed. Scrape sides of processor. Process on high speed for one additional minute. Transfer processed meat to clean small ice cube trays, being careful not to overfill. Place ice cube trays in freezer on level surface. When frozen solid, twist cubes from ice cube trays and place in labeled and dated food storage freezer bag. Place bag in freezer.

Makes approximately 28–42 cubes/servings. Freeze no longer than 3 months.

Toddler Meals

As toddlers, my children really enjoyed eating their homemade food. They would sometimes consume four to five cubes of fruits, veggies and a meat at a *single* sitting. As a result, I came up with some simple meal combination recipes that mix a variety of menu choices with a larger portion size. Taking one prepared toddler meal from your freezer is a lot easier than having to grab 5 to10 different menu items per meal. Also, these single-serving items are easy to take on trips, out to dinner or to the playground.

Toddler Spaghetti

8-10 ounces cooked spaghetti noodles, *cooked, rinsed*
2 cups ground chuck or ground turkey, *cooked, crumbled and drained*
1-2 cups plain tomato spaghetti sauce, *cooked (If bottled, look for low sodium and/or organic varieties.)*
Water

Boil 3 to 4 cups of water on medium heat for approximately 5 minutes, let cool. Place cooked spaghetti noodles in processor with 4 ounces of boiled water. Gradually add additional boiled water as needed being careful not to allow the mixture to become too watery. Process on low speed only until noodles are chopped to small bits. Pour processed noodles into large bowl. Place cooked meat into processor with one cup tomato sauce. Process on low adding additional tomato sauce until mixture processes smoothly to a slightly chunky consistency. Pour processed meat and sauce into large bowl with noodles. Add to your bowl any recipe variations. Mix well. Remove any noticeably large unprocessed portions. Grease or spray muffin tins generously with low fat cooking spray (helps release portions after frozen). Fill each cup in muffin tin 2/3 full (be careful not to overfill). Place muffin trays in freezer on level surface. When frozen solid, gently run warm water along the back of muffin trays. Twist individual muffin portions with your fingers to remove from pan and place in labeled and dated food storage freezer bag. Place bag in freezer.

Variation: Substitute tofu for meat or add 1 cup (or 5 thawed cubes) cooked and processed carrot, squash, sweet potato, zucchini or spinach.

Makes approximately 12-18 portions.

Mini Tuna Casserole

** Some fish including tuna may contain trace amounts of mercury. Consult with your pediatrician regarding the latest feeding guidelines for fish before serving. **

8-10 ounces cooked egg noodles, *cooked, rinsed*
1 small can tuna, *crumbled, drained*
1 small bag frozen peas and carrots, *cooked*
1-2 cans condensed cream of chicken soup, *prepared as directed on can (look for low sodium or organic varieties)*
Water

Boil 3 to 4 cups of water on medium heat for approximately 5 minutes, let cool. Place cooked egg noodles in processor with 4 to 8 ounces ($\frac{1}{2}$-1 cup) of boiled water. Gradually add additional boiled water as needed being careful not to allow the mixture to become too watery. Process on low only until noodles are chopped to small bits. Pour processed noodles into large bowl. Check tuna for choking hazards by mashing with fingers to remove lumps and bones, then add to bowl. Process cooked peas and carrots briefly on low adding boiled water until mixture processes smoothly to a slightly chunky consistency. Add processed peas and carrots to bowl containing noodles and tuna. Add cream of chicken soup. Add to your bowl any recipe variation (see below). Mix gently and thoroughly with a wooden spoon or spatula, removing any large or unprocessed portions. Grease or spray muffin tins generously with low fat cooking spray (helps release portions after frozen). Fill each cup in muffin tin 2/3 full being careful not to overfill. Place muffin trays in freezer on level surface. When frozen solid, gently run warm water along the back of muffin trays. Twist individual muffin portions with your fingers to remove from pan and place in labeled and dated food storage freezer bag. Place bag in freezer.

Variations: $\frac{1}{2}$ cup of cheddar cheese; $\frac{1}{2}$ cup cottage cheese; 1 cup (5 thawed cubes) cooked and processed zucchini or squash.

Makes approximately 12-18 portions

Petite Pot Roast Dinners

** This can easily be made from the leftovers of a family crock pot meal (if it has been prepared without salt, pepper or other spices). **

3 cups cooked, shredded pot roast, *gristle and fat removed*
3 cups cooked carrots, *peeled, sliced* or 1 small bag of frozen carrots, *cooked*
3 large baked potatoes, *skins removed*
3 cups fresh green beans, *ends and strings removed, cooked soft* or 1 small bag frozen green beans, *cooked*
Water or 2 cans low sodium/low fat condensed beef broth

Boil 3 to 4 cups of water on medium heat for approximately 5 minutes, let cool. Place cooked and shredded pot roast in food processor with 4 ounces ($\frac{1}{2}$ cup) of boiled water or one can beef broth. Gradually add additional boiled water as needed, being careful not to allow the mixture to become too watery. Process on low only until pot roast is chopped to small bits. Pour processed roast into large bowl. Process cooked carrots, beans and potatoes in food processor on low along with 4 ounces (1/2 cup) of boiled water, slowly adding boiled water until mixture processes to a slightly chunky consistency. Add water/broth as necessary. Add each processed ingredient to bowl with roast. Add to your bowl any recipe variation (see below). Mix carefully and thoroughly with wooden spoon or spatula, removing any noticeably large or unprocessed portions. Grease or spray muffin tins generously with low fat cooking spray (helps release portions after frozen). Fill each cup in muffin tin 2/3 full being careful not to overfill. Place muffin trays in freezer on level surface. When frozen solid, gently run warm water along the back of muffin trays. Twist individual muffin portions with your fingers to remove from pan and place in labeled and dated food storage freezer bag. Place bag in freezer.

Variations: 1 cup (5 thawed cubes) cooked processed cauliflower, zucchini or squash.

Makes approximately 12-24 portions.

Chicken and Rice Casserole

3 cups cooked chicken breast or roast chicken, *cubed, skin, gristle, bones and fat removed*
3 cups cooked carrots, *peeled, sliced* or 1 small bag of frozen carrots, *cooked*
1 small bag frozen green peas, *cooked*
2-3 cups cooked brown rice *(do not add salt, butter or other spices)*
Water or 2 cans low sodium/low fat condensed chicken broth

Boil 3 to 4 cups of water on medium heat for approximately 5 minutes, let cool. Place cooked, cubed chicken in processor with 4 ounces ($\frac{1}{2}$ cup) of boiled water or 1 can broth. Gradually add additional boiled water/broth as needed being careful not to allow the mixture to become too watery. Process on low only until chicken is chopped to small bits. Pour processed chicken into large bowl. Process cooked carrots, peas and rice on low adding boiled water or broth until mixture processes to a slightly chunky consistency. Add each processed ingredient to bowl with chicken. Add any recipe variations to bowl (see below). Mix carefully and thoroughly with wooden spoon or spatula, removing any noticeably large or unprocessed portions. Grease or spray muffin tins generously with low fat cooking spray (helps release portions after frozen). Fill each cup in muffin tin 2/3 full being careful not to overfill. Place muffin trays in freezer on level surface. When frozen solid, gently run warm water along the back of muffin trays. Twist muffin portions with your fingers to remove from pan and place in labeled and dated food storage freezer bag. Place bag in freezer.

Variations: 4 ounces ($\frac{1}{2}$ cup) shredded cheese; 1 cup (5 thawed cubes) cooked and processed cauliflower, zucchini, broccoli or squash; you may substitute turkey or tofu for chicken.

Makes approximately 12-24 portions.

Christmas • Thanksgiving • Holiday Dinner

** You may substitute any leftover vegetable item from your dinner for any vegetable item in this recipe. Do not include any spicy, heavily salted dishes or any containing un-introduced foods. **

2 cups cooked, cubed/shredded ham or turkey, *skin, gristle, bones and fat removed*
2 cups cooked carrots, *peeled, sliced* or 1 small bag of frozen carrots, *cooked*
2 cups cooked green beans, *ends and strings removed* or 1/2 small bag of frozen green beans, *cooked*
2-3 large baked potatoes or sweet potatoes, *peel potatoes, do not add salt, butter or other spices*
Water or 2 cans low sodium/low fat condensed chicken broth

Boil 3 to 4 cups of water on medium heat for approximately 5 minutes, let cool. Place cooked turkey/ham in processor with 4 ounces ($\frac{1}{2}$ cup) of boiled water or 1 can broth. Process on low only until meat is chopped to small bits. Gradually add additional boiled water/broth as needed being careful not to allow the mixture to become too watery. Pour processed meat into large bowl. Process cooked carrots, green beans and potatoes on low adding boiled water/broth until mixture processes to a slightly chunky consistency. Add each processed ingredient to bowl with turkey. Add any recipe variation to bowl (see below). Mix carefully and thoroughly with wooden spoon or spatula, removing any noticeably large or unprocessed portions. Grease or spray muffin tins generously with low fat cooking spray (helps release portions after frozen). Fill each cup in muffin tin 2/3 full being careful not to overfill. Place muffin trays in freezer on level surface. When frozen solid, gently run warm water along the back of muffin trays. Twist muffin portions with your fingers to remove from pan and place in labeled and dated food storage freezer bag. Place bag in freezer.

Variation: 4 ounces ($\frac{1}{2}$ cup) shredded cheese; 1 cup (5 thawed cubes) cooked and processed cauliflower, zucchini, broccoli or squash; you may substitute chicken for turkey or ham.

Makes approximately 12-24 portions.

Ham, Mac-n-Cheese

2 cups cooked, cubed/shredded ham, *skin, gristle, bones and fat removed*
2 cups cooked zucchini, *peeled, sliced*
2-3 cups cooked elbow macaroni
1 cup shredded cheddar cheese
Water or 2 cans low sodium/low fat condensed broth

Boil 3 to 4 cups of water on medium heat for approximately 5 minutes, let cool. Place cooked ham in processor with 4 ounces ($\frac{1}{2}$ cup) of boiled water or broth. Process on low only until ham is chopped to small bits. Gradually add additional boiled water/ as needed being careful not to allow the mixture to become too watery. Pour processed ham into large bowl. Process cooked zucchini and cooked elbow macaroni on low adding boiled water/ broth until mixture processes to a slightly chunky consistency. Add each processed ingredient to bowl with ham. Add any recipe variations to bowl (see below). Mix carefully and thoroughly with wooden spoon or spatula, removing any noticeably large or unprocessed portions. Grease or spray muffin tins generously with low fat cooking spray (helps release portions after frozen). Fill each cup in muffin tin 2/3 full being careful not to overfill. Place muffin trays in freezer on level surface. When frozen solid, gently run warm water along the back of muffin trays. Twist muffin portions with your fingers to remove from pan and place in labeled and dated food storage freezer bag. Place bag in freezer.

Variation: 1 cup (or 5 thawed cubes) cooked and processed carrots, cauliflower or squash; may substitute chicken or turkey for ham.

Makes approximately 12-24 portions.

Butternut Squash and Beef Barley Meals

2 cups cooked, shredded pot roast or cooked, crumbled lean
ground chuck, *skin, gristle, bones and fat removed*
3-4 cups cooked butternut squash
2 cups cooked barley
Water or 2 cans low sodium/low fat condensed beef broth

Boil 3 to 4 cups of water on medium heat for approximately 5
minutes, let cool. Place cooked, shredded beef in processor with
4 ounces (½ cup) of boiled water or broth. Process on low only
until beef is chopped to small bits. Gradually add additional boiled
water/broth as needed being careful not to allow the mixture
to become too watery. Pour processed beef into large bowl.
Process cooked squash and barley on low adding boiled water/
broth until mixture processes to a slightly chunky consistency.
Add each processed ingredient to bowl with beef. Add any recipe
variation to bowl (see below). Mix carefully with wooden spoon
or spatula, removing any noticeably large or unprocessed portions.
Grease or spray muffin tins generously with low fat cooking
spray (helps release portions after frozen). Fill each cup in muffin
tin 2/3 full being careful not to overfill. Place muffin trays in
freezer on level surface. When frozen solid, gently run warm
water along the back of muffin trays. Twist muffin portions
with your fingers to remove from pan and place in labeled and
dated food storage freezer bag. Place bag in freezer.

Variations: 1 cup (or 5 thawed cubes) cooked and processed
zucchini; 4 ounces (½ cup) cooked and processed carrots; 4 ounces
(½ cup) cooked prunes.

Makes approximately 12-24 portions.

Finger Foods and Menu Extras

The following foods are not only healthy and nutritious but some can really help with your child's burgeoning interest in self-feeding. Try adding one of these foods periodically to your child's menu. Remember to follow the 3-4 day rule between the introduction of all new foods and watch for the signs of allergic reaction. Also, never let your child eat even finger foods unattended. Monitor your child closely and always be on the lookout for signs of choking.

- Cooked soft brown rice
- Cooked soft barley
- Navy or pinto beans (cooked soft)
- Cooked elbow macaroni
- Tofu (cut into small chunks)
- Shredded Cheese
- Fresh served fruits: watermelon (seeded and diced), cantaloupe (diced)
- Soft, diced cooked carrots/peas
- Soft, diced cooked pears/peaches (peeled, pits/cores removed)
- Cooked diced apples (peeled, cores removed)
- Jello cubes
- Puffed Rice or Wheat

Due to the possibility of sensitivities or allergic reaction, wait until on or around your child's first birthday and consult with your pediatrician before serving the following food items:

- Scrambled eggs (small chunks)
- Flakes of cooked fish (carefully de-bone)
- Homemade puddings
- Mandarin oranges

Tapioca Dessert

** For children who may have a sensitivity to milk and/or egg whites, please consult with your pediatrician before serving. **

4-6 cups of prepared small pearl Tapioca, *prepare according to directions*
1 cup water/milk/formula

Prepare small pearl Tapioca according to directions on box. If too thick to pour from pan, add ½-1 cup water/milk or formula. Pour immediately into clean *small* ice cube trays being careful not to overfill. Place ice cube trays in freezer on level surface. When frozen solid, twist cubes from ice cube trays and place in labeled and dated food storage freezer bag. Place bag in freezer.

Variation: Serve warm mixed with 1 thawed, cube blackberry/ blueberry or raspberry. YUM!

Makes approximately 28-42 servings

Sample Toddler Menus

DAY 1

Breakfast: Banana-Plum Cream of Wheat

Snack: Peach Yogurt (1 cube peaches with plain unsweetened yogurt)

Lunch: Cooked soft Navy Beans, 1 cube Peas, 1 cube Carrots

Snack: Diced Watermelon

Dinner: Chicken and Rice Dinner, 1 cube Apples

DAY 2

Breakfast: Scrambled egg with 1/8 cup shredded cheese

Snack: Soft diced cooked Apples/Pears with Multi-Grain Oat Cereal

Lunch: 1 cube Turkey, 1 cube Peas, 1 tablespoon prepared Pastina

Snack: Mandarin Oranges

Dinner: Butternut Squash and Beef Barley Meals with 1 cube Tapioca Dessert

---

DAY 3

Breakfast: Pear-Mango Rice Cereal

Snack: Toast Triangles and cooked Carrots

Lunch: Green Pea Cottage Cheese, cooked soft Beans

Snack: 2 ounces (1/8th cup) shredded Cheese

Dinner: Squashy Pork (1 cube squash, 1 cube Cauliflower, 1 cube Carrot, 1 cube Pork.)

DAY 4

Breakfast: Pruney-Apple Oatmeal Cereal

Snack: Rice Cake

Lunch: 1 cube Turkey, 1 cube Sweet Potato and Green Bean Pastina

Snack: Diced Cantaloupe

Dinner: Toddler Spaghetti

DAY 5

Breakfast:	Plum, Pear and Blackberry Yogurt
Snack:	Cooked Peas
Lunch:	Broccoli, Cauliflower and Potato Medley
Snack:	1 cube Prunes, 1 cube Apples
Dinner:	Ham Mac-n-Cheese

DAY 6

Breakfast:	Scrambled Egg with diced Tofu
Snack:	1 cube Mango
Lunch:	1 cube Sweet Potato, 1 cube Green Bean, Cooked Elbow Macaroni
Snack:	Cottage Cheese
Dinner:	Mini Tuna Casserole

DAY 7

Breakfast:	Banana, Blueberry Oatmeal
Snack:	Shredded or diced Cheese
Lunch:	Squash Cottage Cheese with Toast Triangles
Snack:	Apple-Pear-Peach Medley
Dinner:	Petite Pot Roast Dinner

Tips for Travel

Tips for Travel

Whether you are planning an extended vacation, or simply contemplating dinner in a local restaurant, traveling with your baby does not require you to resort to the baby food aisle at the supermarket. Most of your homemade frozen baby foods will last 24 hours if kept cold … longer if kept frozen. If you are unable to take along a cooler or small insulated lunchbox, you might consider investing in a "mini" food processor (readily available for about $10.00). My "mini" went with us everywhere we traveled when the kids were young. Small and portable, a mini processor allows you to instantly grind up adult meals or make small baby food batches you can store in the refrigerator. If on an extended vacation, a "mini" processor can easily process canned fruits/vegetables or small batches of cooked items for freezing or refrigeration. If in a pinch and using canned foods for processing, try to avoid fruits with added sugar/syrup and look for vegetables packed in water/low sodium varieties.

Going to a restaurant or on a play date does not have to be an ordeal with your own prepared, frozen meals. An insulated lunchbox or bottle cooler will hold several menu choices at the proper temperature until mealtime.

Afterward

When my pediatrician announced it was time to move beyond formula, my first scouting trip to the grocery store for "baby food" was mind boggling. I began to notice there were preservatives and additives in many "ready to eat" snacks, foods and desserts. However, instead of feeling forced to always purchase these foods for my growing children, I began to experiment with preparing my own. I became knowledgeable about nutrition and gained confidence in my cooking abilities. Now, as they rocket through toddler-hood and enter school cafeterias, I continue to have the confidence to prepare fresh and healthful menus and to work as an advocate for healthy, natural menu choices in our public and private schools.

The media proclaims childhood obesity is on the rise. You only have to pay attention at school or at the mall to know this is true. I hope this book will help you gain the confidence to begin preparing good, healthful meals for your babies.

It is never too early or too late to take an active role in providing your children with a solid foundation for a healthy lifestyle.

Good luck and good eating!

Acknowlegements

The helping hands and supportive hearts of so many people touched the writing and making of this cookbook. I endeavor to thank you all, whether here or in person. For my wonderful husband Russ and all our children, Paige, Phoebe, Steven, Matthew, Stephanie, Jerome and William – giving me the gift of motherhood has been an incredible adventure and journey. Thank you. To my own "mothers", Lindell and Bonnie, who have taught me how to use the gift of motherhood. No mother has had finer role models and life models than the two of you. For the many mothers that helped, collaborated and further inspired me to share this book with you: My illustrator Sheri Lawrence, editor Nancy Schneider, my Aunt and author Gayle Bartos-Pool, and my friend and pediatrician Brenda McGhee, all of whom cheerfully volunteered to share their many god-given talents with me to create this book. To the mothers of MCF (Mothers' Christian Fellowship) who have lent their shoulders for burden sharing, arms for hugs and hearts for loving support, my love and appreciation always. Thank you to my long-time best friends (now mothers themselves): Mindy, Martha and LaVonne who each long ago left their footprints on my heart.

INDEX*

About the Author: Julianne E. Hood lives in Northeast Ohio. She and her husband, Rusty are parents of two daughters ages six and four. She is a graduate of Furman University in Greenville, South Carolina and The Case Western Reserve University School of Law in Cleveland, Ohio. She was a trial lawyer for seven years before beginning her second career as a stay-at-home Mom. In addition to her passion for making homemade baby food, Julianne  enjoys sewing (particularly baby blankets and toddler clothes), reading, gardening, computers and every aspect of being a "mommy." She and her husband are active members of their church and are licensed foster/foster to adopt parents. This is her first book.

 Dr. Brenda McGhee is a board certified pediatrician at Dr. Senders & Associates, a nationally known, award-winning pediatric practice in University Heights, Ohio, well-known for its strong commitment to parent education. (www.drsenders.com). A graduate of Wright State University School of Medicine who completed her pediatric residency at Rainbow Babies and Children's Hospital in Cleveland, Ohio, she is also an active educator and Clinical Preceptor for Case Western Reserve School of Medicine. She is a highly regarded lecturer on pediatrics and has offered expert advice throughout the community and on television. She enjoys cooking (cheddar cheese and French onion soups are among her favorites), but sticks to old-fashioned dog food for her two Newfoundlands and a Labrador Retriever.

Printed in the United States
114668LV00008B/261/A